SHARKS

D1372308

SHARKS

BY SARAH R. RIEDMAN

Illustrated with photographs,
and map by Robert McGlynn

AN EASY-READ FACT BOOK
FRANKLIN WATTS I NEW YORK I LONDON I 1977

Library of Congress Cataloging in Publication Data
Riedman, Sarah Regal, 1902-
    Sharks.

    (An Easy-read fact book)
    Includes index.
    SUMMARY: Describes the physical characteristics and
habits of sharks and their relatives and discusses
myths about them.
    1. Sharks—Juvenile literature. [1. Sharks]
I. McGlynn, Robert.   II. Title.
QL638.9.R545   597'.31   77-5171
ISBN 0-531-01314-6

R.L. 2.9 Spache Modified Formula
EDL Core Vocabulary

This is a **shark.** It is a fish. But not like any you have for dinner.

Almost all sharks are saltwater fish. They live in all oceans. But mostly they like warm waters.

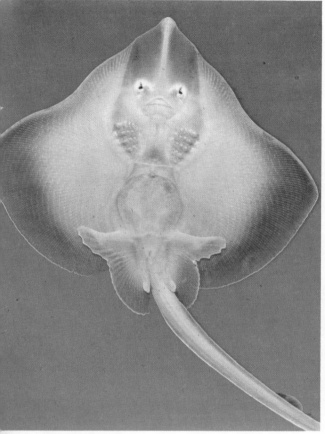 

Skate   **Electric ray**

Sharks come in all sizes, and many have unusual shapes. Some in the shark family do not look at all like sharks.

Cownosed ray

There are shark cousins called **skates** and **rays.** The
spiny dogfish is a small shark, about a foot (30 cm.) long.
The **great white shark** may be 25 feet (8 m.) long.

There are two really big sharks. The **basking shark** is 40 feet (12 m.) long. And the **whale shark** is 60 feet (18 m.) long. But these are not dangerous to people. Why? Because they have no big teeth. Their very tiny teeth are useless. And they don't eat meat.

The mouth of a basking shark

This sand shark shows its fin shaped like a triangle.

When a shark swims, all we see above the water is a fin. Its shape is a triangle. It is made of something we call **cartilage** (CART-ill-edge). It can bend, but not break.

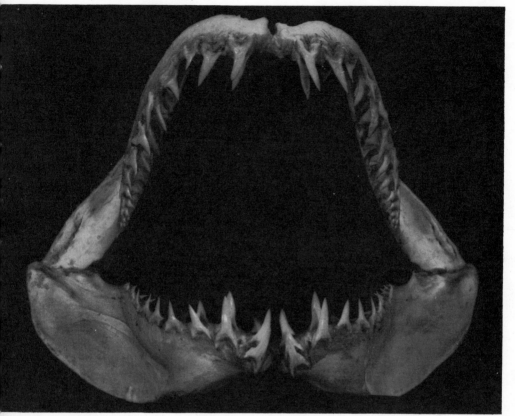

Sand tiger shark jawbone and teeth

The strange thing about a shark is that its whole skeleton is cartilage. A shark has not one bone in its body. Even its teeth are cartilage covered with a stone-hard material.

Look how big the mako shark's mouth is.

See how big the shark's mouth is when the jaws are open. The teeth are usually in four or five rows. When one row wears out, those teeth drop off. The row behind it moves up. A new one grows in its place.

Sharkskin is rough like sandpaper. It is covered with tiny shark teeth. They are called **denticles** (DENT-uh-culs) or "skin teeth."

This white shark gets oxygen from the water.

**The tiger shark's gill slits
are next to its side fins.**

Like other fish, a shark needs oxygen to live. It gets
oxygen from the water around it.

The water comes through two tiny holes, one on
each side of the head, as well as through the mouth.
It passes over the **gills** and flows out through the **gill
slits.**

Would you believe that a shark swims to breathe? Swimming makes the water move. The water flows into the mouth while the shark swims. If the shark stopped to rest, it would sink and die.

Most sharks are built for fast swimming. Like a torpedo it streaks through the water. The back fin keeps the shark steady. It uses other fins to steer. It uses its tail to move forward.

Like all sharks, nurse sharks use their fins to steer.

The mako shark is the best swimmer.

The best swimmer is the **mako** (MAH-koh) **shark.** For a short time it can swim at 40 miles (64 km.) an hour.

Sharks are fierce, hungry eaters.

Most of all, sharks are fierce, hungry hunters. With teeth as sharp as razors, they rip, tear, and slash their food.

The nurse shark feeds on slow animals.

Sharks hunt for large fish, turtles, sea birds, and seals. They also eat other sharks, skates, and rays. Even dead ones are food. This helps keep the ocean clean.

Not all sharks are good swimmers. Some are slow-moving. They go after different food on the sea floor. They feed on slow animals. They have teeth made for crushing hard shells. They eat clams, oysters, lobsters, crabs, and water snakes.

The sawfish is also part of the shark family.

**The basking shark is very big.
But it eats only plankton.**

The basking and whale sharks have enormous mouths, but no useful teeth. They scoop up tons of tiny floating animals and plants. These plants and animals are called **plankton.**

How do sharks find their food?

Tests show that a shark can smell, taste, see, hear, and feel. Mostly sharks find food by smelling it even far away.

Lemon shark

A shark has two nostrils in front of its mouth. As it swims, water enters the nostrils. The smell of food in the water reaches the shark.

Fishermen call sharks "swimming noses." You can see why.

Sharks have very small eyes. How well can they see?

In one test a shark's nostrils were plugged. It could not smell. Then bait was put into the tank. The shark went straight for it. It was able to see well enough.

Here you can see the shark's
nostrils, eyes, gill slits, and mouth.

What can a shark see?

It does not see color. It does not see specks of things. But it sees anything moving, even at night or in cloudy water.

Sharks see quite well.

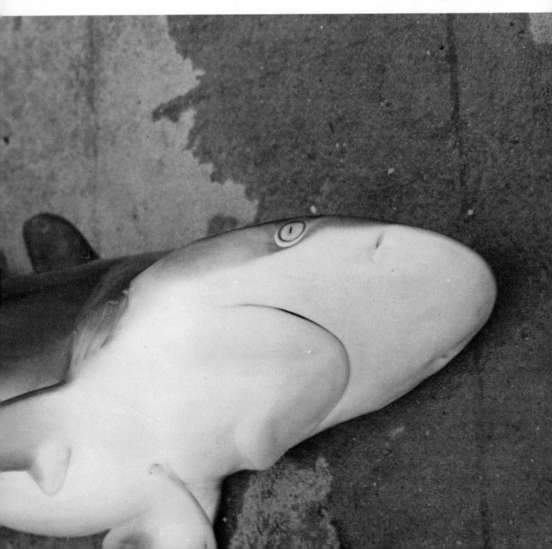

As you see, sharks do not have ears like we do.

Does a shark hear?

It does not have ears like you do. And what is there to hear in the ocean? A struggling fish makes noise. A person swimming makes noise. We know that sharks swim toward these sounds. They can hear quite well.

Watch a shark swimming in an **aquarium** (ah-KWEAR-e-um). It does not hit the wall. It stays out of the way of big rocks. And it keeps its balance as well as you do. How?

Sharks have little canals filled with fluid. These canals are for balance. From snout to tail sharks have these canals under the skin. As the shark swims, it stirs up the fluid.

If the shark swims near a big rock, it can feel the water bouncing against the rock. The shark then steers away from it.

All sharks can steer away from rocks easily. This is a sand shark.

So, the shark has many senses. But one sense is strangely missing.

A shark does not seem to feel pain. A badly hurt shark keeps on eating. People have seen it eat its own insides, trailing out of its body. Eating is what the shark must do even when it is almost dead.

All shark babies start from eggs. The male shark puts sperm inside the body of the female shark. There the sperm joins the eggs, which become fertile.

Some sharks drop the fertile eggs in the ocean. But each shark egg is inside an **egg case** or **envelope.** The tough egg case protects the egg.

These are egg cases of a skate.

The egg case protects the fertile eggs.

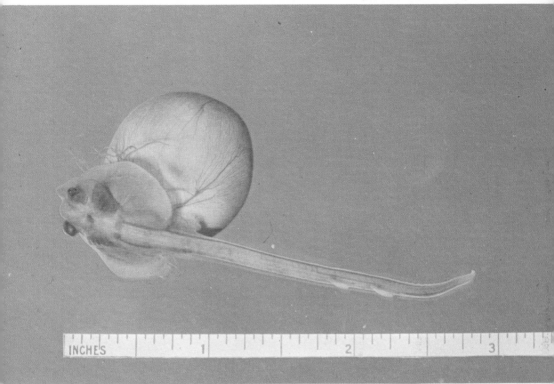

A skate embryo, seven weeks old.

The growing baby shark is called the **embryo**
(EM-bree-oh). It feeds on the yolk or yellow of the
egg. It gets oxygen from seawater. The water flows
into the egg case through tiny openings. The waste
gas leaves through the same tiny holes.

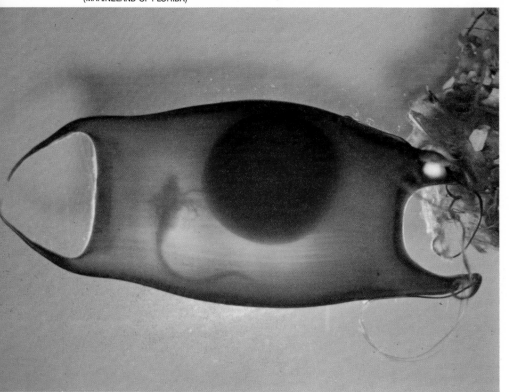

**You can see the embryo
inside the skate egg case.**

When the embryo has become a baby shark, it gets out of the egg case.

All skates hatch this way. And so does the giant whale shark.

Most sharks, however, develop in another way.

The fertile eggs, each in its case, stay inside the female. When the food is used up, the baby shark hatches out. It leaves the mother's body, ready to swim and eat on its own.

All skates hatch from egg cases. This is a clearnosed skate.

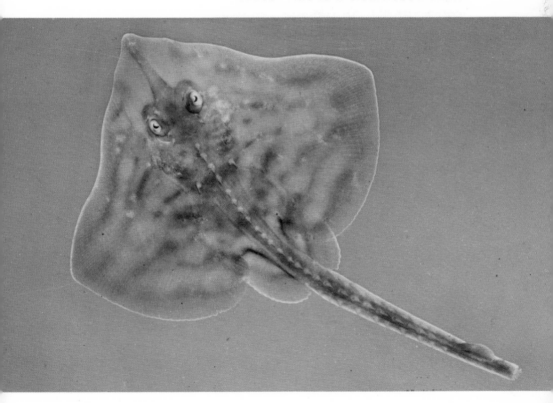

In still other sharks, the mako and **sand sharks**, the embryo eats up all the yolk. But it is not yet ready to live on its own. It then feeds on a kind of "milk" made by the mother. When ready to live by itself the baby shark leaves.

Baby sharks must swim away in a hurry. If they don't, the mother shark may eat them. She is not "mad" at them, just very hungry.

Egg cases wash up on the beach.　　　　**Shark babies**

(MARINELAND OF FLORIDA)　　　　　　　(MARINELAND OF FLORIDA)

(34)

Most shark babies hatch inside
the mother's body. Then they
come out into the water.

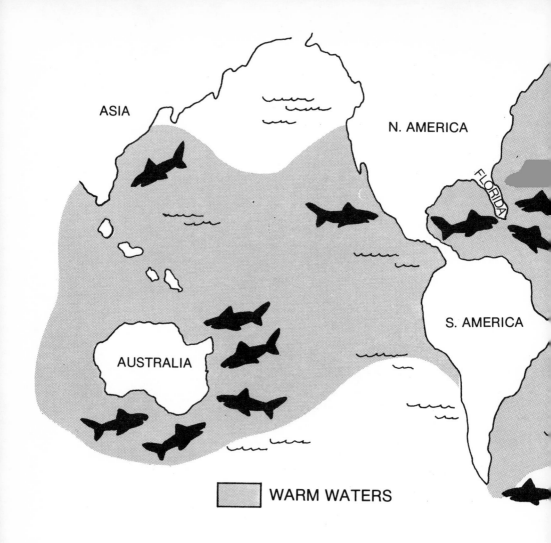

ASIA

N. AMERICA

FLORIDA

S. AMERICA

AUSTRALIA

WARM WATERS

Do sharks bite people?

A hungry shark will bite into anything: a boat, life raft, water ski, or a person. But only the great white shark is called a **man-eater.**

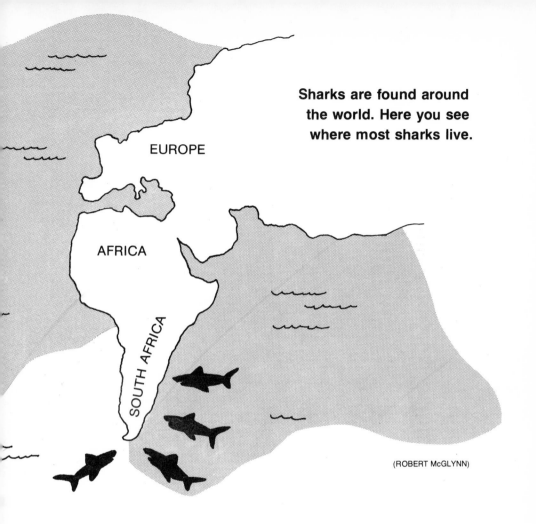

Sharks are found around the world. Here you see where most sharks live.

EUROPE

AFRICA

SOUTH AFRICA

(ROBERT McGLYNN)

The waters most crowded with sharks are around Australia, South Africa, and Florida. People also crowd in these places to swim, surf, and skin dive. That is why most shark attacks happen there.

There are more shark attacks in summer, and more in daytime, when most people swim.

Sharks are dangerous. To keep out of danger where sharks live, people follow these rules of safety:

If someone yells: "SHARK," leave the water.
Don't swim alone; always swim with an adult.
Don't try to swim in cloudy water.
If you have a small bleeding cut, stay out.
Don't drag a freshly hooked fish in the water.
Remember how well a shark can smell.

These are rules for swimmers to remember.

Sharks are dangerous.

**Sharks are eaten in
many parts of the world.**

In many parts of the world people eat shark meat. It makes good eating, fried, baked , or as a fishburger. In England shark meat is used in fish and chips. In China the shark fins make tasty soup.

**Sharkskin makes
strong leather.**

Other parts of sharks are useful, too. The skin makes
strong leather. Shark-liver oil is used to soften
leather. It also polishes wood, goes into paints, and
greases machinery.

Not everything you hear about sharks is true. Have you heard that:

- A shark has to turn on its back to eat?
- Sharks eat iron nails, tin cans, and rubber tires?
- It is safer to swim at night, because sharks don't eat at night?
- Sharks always attack dolphins?
- Sharks have no animal friends?

Don't believe any of these things because:

- A shark snaps its food as it swims, with its belly down.
- Sharks cannot eat tin cans anymore than you can. They may swallow tin cans. But they will vomit them up again.

- Sharks feed anytime, day or night. Few people swim at night. So there are few attacks at night.

- In the open sea, hungry sharks attack dolphins. But not in an aquarium, because they are well fed.

The diver is safe from this hammerhead shark. The shark is well fed.

**The remora is built to
hold on to other fish.**

● One kind of fish sharks do not eat is the **remora.** A
remora hitches a ride on the shark's body. It eats
animal pests that stick to the shark's skin and gills.
While eating and helping the shark, the remora is
also protected from enemies.

- The fish that swim close are called **pilot fish.** Some people say that pilot fish lead the shark to food. But sharks don't need help to find food, as we have seen. So sharks and these fish are just friendly neighbors.

This lemon shark has many neighbors. Pilot fish and remora are not afraid of it.

INDEX

ABOUT THE AUTHOR

Sarah R. Riedman is no stranger to books for young
readers. She has written over thirty in the last thirty
years, in addition to her work as editor, college
professor in biology, physiology, and hygiene, and
author of college textbooks and adult books. Since
moving to Jensen Beach, Florida, she has become
increasingly interested in the marine life of her
adopted home. Florida is one of the three leading
shark-infested areas, and because of this, Ms.
Riedman's interest in sharks, and the fact and fiction
being written about them, heightened her feeling for
the need of a book about sharks for the young
reader.